The
RusticHome

The RusticHome

Written & Photographed by

Ralph Kylloe

GIBBS SMITH
TO ENRICH AND INSPIRE HUMANKIND

Paperback Edition
15 14 13 12 11   5 4 3 2 1

Text © 2006 Ralph Kylloe
Photographs © 2006 Ralph Kylloe

Published by
Gibbs Smith
P.O. Box 667
Layton, Utah 84041

1.800.835.4993 orders
www.gibbs-smith.com

Designed by Adrienne Pollard
Printed and bound in China

Gibbs Smith books are printed on either recycled, 100% post-consumer
waste, FSC-certified papers or on paper produced from sustainable
PEFC-certified forest/controlled wood source. Learn more at
www.pefc.org.

Library of Congress Cataloging-in-Publication Data

Kylloe, Ralph R.
  The rustic home / Ralph Kylloe ; photographs by Ralph Kylloe.
     p. cm.
  ISBN 978-1-58685-810-0 (hardcover)
  ISBN 978-1-4236-2341-0 (paperback)
  1. Country homes—West (U.S.) I. Title.

NA7561.K95 2006
728'.37—dc22

                                    2006013466

For my wife, Michele, the greatest lady to ever walk the planet!

Contents

THIS HAS BEEN MY MOST COMPLICATED BOOK to date. In truth, there have been more people involved in this book than I initially planned. The reason for that is that I had to travel farther and I have included significantly more information in the captions and text than I have in my other books. I tried to acknowledge as many people as possible—because they deserve it.

But I'm going to be honest here. I can't include all of the information I collected nor acknowledge everyone who was instrumental in the completion of this book. There were many days when I would wander through construction sites and chat with masons, carpenters, electricians, designers and many others involved. Their input and their ability to put things in plain English so that I could understand what I was looking at was invaluable. Truthfully, the people who both design and build these homes are artists in the truest sense. The world is a more beautiful place because of their efforts.

Frankly, on many days I made a pest out of myself in the office of architect Larry Pearson. I bothered just about everybody while they tried to complete their assigned tasks. Just to mention a few: Queen Jacque, Dennis, Amanda, Boone, Keith, Chas, Katie, Greg, Josh, Ben, Phill, and even Alyssa, the office receptionist, who saved my neck several times by resolving my computer problems. I'm lucky no one clobbered me as I succeeded on many occasions in disrupting the normal work flow.

There are many people to thank for their help with this book. In my other books I've thanked everyone who has ever lived and is presently living because that leaves out no one. And no one can say that I forgot to mention this or that individual. That acknowledgement seemed to work, as I was only bombarded with a few nasty comments from some disappointed individual who felt he or she should have been mentioned. So I'll repeat myself again: many thanks to everyone in the entire world, including the dead, the living and all of those not yet born. Thank you for your help with this book!

On the other hand, I specifically acknowledge the owners of the homes pictured in this book. As a rule, I never identify the owners or where the home is located. It makes life much easier. Nonetheless, I must clearly state my abounding appreciation to the owners of these homes. Each of the owners who gave their permission was gracious, courteous and more helpful than they will ever know. I thank each of you. And if ever any of you need someone to spend a week in your home (especially during fishing season), just let me know because I'll be there in a second and I promise to pick up after myself!

I must also personally thank Larry Pearson. For my taste, you're the best in the business and you've brought the entire realm of rustic design and architecture to new heights! I also want to thank architect Kirk Michels of Livingston, Montana, and architect Janet Jarvis of Ketchum, Idaho. Your homes are also extraordinary! I must also mention Harry Howard of Yellowstone Traditions. Harry has on many occasions been a tremendous help to me and my efforts by unselfishly offering his time and knowledge. And he's a pretty good fly fisherman and a great artist as well. Also Chris Lohss of Lohss Construction spent several days with me giving tours of his exceptional projects and helping me lug heavy photo equipment through mountains of unforgiving snow.

I must also thank my editor, Madge Baird. How she tolerates me I'll never know. But she always makes me look good and for that I'm forever thankful. Also many thanks to my publisher, Gibbs Smith. His vision has allowed individuals like me and many other authors to document the ongoing evolution of the rustic culture. Equally important is my wife, Michele. I could not do what I do without her. We make a great team and I promise to do more of the household chores once this book is complete. And to my wonderful daughter, Lindsey—Cutie Pie, you're the greatest!

Here's a few other individuals I want to thank:

LPAIA (Bozeman	Dennis Derham	Carson Monson
LPAIA (Big Fork)	Coley Heiser	Shelby Rose
Adam Britt	Amanda Ingraham	Alyssa Ruffie
Keith Anderson	Patrick Johanson	Zack Spencer
Phill Ballard	Ben Kennedy	Jacque Spitler
Josh Barr	Carol Lehmann	Jed Thomas
Chas Bolin	Boone Lennon	Justin Tollefson
Tad Bradley	Katie Lineberger	
Josh Burden	Greg Matthews	

THIS IS MY SEVENTEENTH BOOK. It seems like a lot. But it's my life's work. And I have more ideas rolling around in my head than I have time left. In truth, I didn't complete my first book until I was in my mid-forties. I was a late bloomer. I could have done more with my life, but right now I'm not doing so bad. For me, it does not get any easier with each new book.

This has been the hardest one so far. I've had to travel more and a few glitches have prevented me from completing this book sooner. But with its publication, I'm on to a new project. I think I'm a better photographer than I was a few years ago, and a better writer; that's the nature of growth. The more you do it, the better you get at it—at least in theory anyway. Enough of that kind of stuff for now.

The rustic market continues to grow. Looking at it as a lifes pan, the style of Rustic is now in young adulthood. Rustic furniture builders are better today than they have ever been. Architects working in the medium are exploring new venues within the field, and builders of rustic homes are now doing incredible work. But as with all fields of endeavor, the work of a few exceptional individuals rises to the top, and the homes you'll see in the following pages showcase some of the best work in the rustic field today.

Rustic arts are enjoying incredible popularity at this point in our history. More than ten thousand log homes are exported to Japan every year. Thousands more each year are constructed here in America. At my gallery in Lake George, New York, each year I receive a hundred or so packages or emails from young rustic furniture builders eager to jump on the bandwagon. But as with budding artists, few ever reach the top. It's the same with architects, painters, homebuilders, etc. I look for originality, craftsmanship and a lot of other things. But my point is that more and more people are finding real joy in the pursuit of the inherent beauty in the rustic arts. And there is honor in trying. There is no honor not trying. This applies to everything.

Here's another consideration: the third period of the rustic arts, the period we are in now, is about fifteen years old. The first period was from about the 1880s to about 1910. That's when the Adirondack Great Camp movement took hold. The second was in the early 1930s. Many new hickory furniture companies, as well as the western Molesworth movement, took off. The third period really seriously began in the early 1990s. Today there are more companies manufacturing rustic furniture, building log homes and engaging in related ventures than I can possibly keep track of. Some say that interest in rustic is a fad or a trend. I disagree. I consider it a complete lifestyle, or a movement in itself. The reason I

mention this is because the public today is recognizing the inherent value and beauty in all things rustic. The reasons rustic furniture builders are better today than ever before is that several very talented people have entered the field, and many who have been in the business for a long time are refining their skills. Some architects are pushing the envelope when it comes to innovation and design, and many log home builders are very sophisticated in their approach to construction techniques.

I've spent thirty years in the rustic business. It's not what I planned on doing, but sometimes you just have to go where the river pushes you. And I've loved just about every second of my life and career. It's true that I've had squabbles with some people in my lifetime. This happens to everyone. No one gets along with everybody. You can't make everyone happy in the world. Frankly, some people are just jerks. But I've always respected sincere effort and I've always recognized talent and ability. And I give credit where credit is due. But in my books I can't include everyone and there are many out there with great talent who have not yet been noticed or recognized by the public. Hopefully, in time, they will be.

And so I continue with my effort to document and popularize the Rustic Arts movement. I've written about all kinds of subjects related to rustic endeavors. The artists in the field continue to both amaze and thrill me with their latest creations. That's how it should be. People grow, and so do their talents. It's not about money. It's not about impressing others. It's about developing one's skills and talents. It's about achieving one's potential. It's about creating great art. It's about the little chills I get when I see something really great. It's about the mysterious thrills and passions of art. It's about little steps forward. It's about becoming a better person. And all that can be achieved by trying to bring everything you do up to the level of the artistic. It's not easy. Some things are really boring. Some things are really insignificant. But if people keep art in the back of their minds and try to achieve something wonderful with each endeavor, then life becomes both meaningful and wonderful.

This book, in a small way, is about that process. At least to me it is.

Many of my previous books have been about rustic architecture. The books have sold well. I continue to find new examples of rustic everything. I've wanted to do another book on rustic architecture for some time and have looked at more homes than I care to remember. But I keep coming back to one architect: Larry Pearson of Bozeman, Montana. I actually made it a point to find other homes outside of the Montana vernacular rustic home. But I keep coming back to Larry. And so I give enormous credit to this one guy. But, in truth, that is an incorrect and incomplete statement. A home is not the effort of one individual. An architect can only provide a plan. It takes the talent of dozens of others, including engineers, carpenters, electricians, masons, painters, roofers, landscapers, interior designers, and on and on to create a great home. It also takes the vision of the homeowner to encourage and allow others to create. (And to pay the bills!) So this is not a book about Larry. He is, however, the composer of a great symphony and conductor of a great orchestra. But he is only as good as the musicians that surround him. This is a book about the ongoing evolution of a great movement and the people who make it happen.

Frankly, and I'll let down my guard here, I love this stuff. I actually giggle quietly to myself when I see great homes and great art. It is the closest I can get to a spiritual experience. It's a heavenly, joyous experience for me to tour these homes. And, although I am fully aware of the limitations of photography, I hope that even in just a small way, the people who look at this book will find just a sliver of joy in the images I present on these pages.

About the Homes

Rustic homes are undergoing a dramatic evolution these days. Some traditional homes offer just a few hickory rockers on their front porches. Many homeowners are adding an Adirondack room to their settings. Others are adding just a few high-end pieces placed alongside their traditional furniture. Other people are building complete log homes and filling them with traditional furniture. And others still, whom I affectionately refer to as extremists, are building extraordinary rustic homes and filling them with either quintessential traditional or rustic furniture. This book contains examples of each of the above.

Many of the homes presented here have "knocked me out." Some are so extraordinary that I've just wandered through them for a few hours, marveling at the grandiose design, architecture, furnishings and stunning views. I would happily live in any of the homes shown in this book. The home that shocked me the most, however, is what I first took to be just another five-million-dollar ski house on top of a great mountain. Upon entering the home, it was very apparent that this was an ultra-modern George Jetson fifties home that was unique in design and originality. This home "pushed the envelope" of modern rustic design and I felt compelled to offer it in this publication.

So my intent with this book is to show numerous examples of how creative and innovative individuals can be when it comes to rustic design and to further document the ongoing evolution within this style. Hope you like it!

INTRODUCTION

RUSTIC HOMES ARE NOT NEW. Neither are they the advent of Adirondackers, Native Americans, or imported Americans, for that matter. The earliest known examples of log homes in North America are from the Northeast Territories. There, examples of stacked, driftwood log structures have been unearthed that date back as early as 3000 b.c.

There is, at the same time, significant evidence of log structures in the Mesolithic cultures of peoples from the Northern European and Asiatic regions dating back to 10,000 b.c. And from earlier still are sites unearthed in Russia that contained shelters made of stacked mammoth bones! So, rustic shelters and log homes are not new. They've been with us for a while.

There is another misconception regarding log homes that should be addressed. The first Europeans that arrived on our shores did not build log cabins. Most of the very early structures erected were horrible shacks that quickly fell apart, tents or other transient structures that did little to insulate and protect recent arrivals from Europe. But as society took hold, structures were built that reflected the cultures to which immigrants were accustomed. One does not think of Plymouth Rock or Boston or Philadelphia or St. Augustine, Florida (the first city in America) as towns made of log cabins. Further, records indicate that there were no log homes

in Virginia until more than a century after the creation of Jamestown. However, with the immigration of Swedes, Dutch, Finns, English, Irish, Germans, Swiss and many others into North America, the westward exodus of humanity began. And the one material that was constant from the Eastern Seaboard to the dregs of Death Valley was trees.

But consider this for a moment. Not surprisingly, because of the nomadic nature of Native Americans, the idea of permanent log cabins never caught on. The reason that Native Americans failed to have permanent housing is because, along with their nomadic lifestyles, they did not have the appropriate tools to construct homes from materials that were theirs for the taking. True, they had hatchets and battle axes, but these implements were created from stones, not iron. They could cut meat, but their instruments, which dulled almost immediately, were no match for trees that needed repeated blows to fell.

Interestingly enough, the original ax brought over from Europe was first designed during the Stone Age and with a few modifications during the Bronze and Iron ages, lasted unchanged for almost 10,000 years. Designed and used mostly as a weapon, the ax of old was appropriate for cracking skulls and was less then perfect when used as a tool for the building of homes!

And then around 1740 the English improved on the design and called their new tool the "American ax." Instead of just three pounds, the new ax weighed up to seven pounds and more, and the steel blade could be sharpened with just a whetstone! The opposite end of the blade was flat and could be used to both hammer nails and pound stakes into the ground. In America, manufacturers of the ax used hickory poles—the strongest and toughest wood in the country—as handles for their hatchets and axes. The tool was an immediate success and no self-respecting pioneer could be without one. Far more than the gun, it was the ax that helped settle the West! From then on, log cabins became the norm in the interior of the country. Newspaper clippings from numerous regions around the country document the rise of the log cabin in North America. One Ohio historian wrote that "the dwellings of the pioneers of the Western Reserve . . . consisted solely of log cabins." In 1796, regarding the state of Tennessee, Thomas Dillon wrote that "there are no buildings in this State . . . but Log Cabins!" The march was on!

Log cabins were the preferred home of the pioneers for several reasons. One, they were easy to build. Trees were everywhere and the new tools allowed for easy and affordable access to building materials. (The record for three men constructing a single-room log cabin complete with chimney and fireplace is presently three days! In general a single individual, without getting fancy can build a simple one-room log cabin in a week or two.) Further, these homes protected families from not only environmental concerns but irate neighbors and unhappy Native Americans as well! Initially, cabins were constructed without windows, mainly because glass was hard to get and easily broken. Often, however, window openings were covered with animal skins to keep out the insects and maundering animals! Later on, paper smeared with animal grease covered window openings and kept out the rain and allowed the entry of at least some light to brighten the home.

Front doors were usually made of heavy slabs of wood and always opened out rather than in. They were hung with leather straps or wooden hinges. A latch and crossbar were secured on the inside of the door and, at the very least, provided minimal protection from intruders. Sometimes a loft that served as sleeping quarters for kids was created on the interior of the building.

The fireplace was the heart of the home. Winters were often long and brutal and fireplaces brought families together by providing both warmth and light. Later on, cast-iron stoves were introduced that facilitated both cooking and heating. Stones for the fireplaces were almost always dug from the ground immediately surrounding the home.

The earliest log homes always had notched corners. Nails were not available in the wilderness and builders quickly became quite skilled at cutting notches on the ends of the logs that allowed such logs to be "locked" together. Several types of notching—including full dovetailing, V-notch, square notch, half notch, diamond notch, half dovetail and double notching—evolved through this early period of American history and examples of such construction can be seen on many early log homes.

But logs are organic and uneven. When you stack logs on top of each other, significant space remains between them. And that space needs to be filled to keep out the hostile elements and bugs and to keep the interior of the building warm. So, to fill the cracks in

early homes, all sorts of materials were used to seal the structure, including small twigs, stones, moss and other debris. To further seal the cracks, mud, wet clay mixed with animal fur or straw, and all sorts of other stuff was applied to offer protection from the elements. Initially this process was known as "daubing" or "chinking."

To complete the early log homes, builders often covered the roofs with two to three layers of log planks and sealed them with materials similar to what had been used to seal the log walls. Occasionally, early settlers would sod the roof first with a layer of dirt and then seed it to allow all sorts of grasses to grow, thus providing protection from the elements and a further layer of insulation for the cold months.

Furnishings for early log homes were often primitive at best. Materials for furniture were acquired from the immediate surroundings. Mattresses were stuffed with straw and many other types of organic material. Furniture was created from branches and tree limbs. And sanitary facilities were just out the front door! At the same time, historical log homes are easy to both date and identify by their materials and contents. For instance, lodgepole pine trees common in the Rocky Mountains were obviously never used in the East. Homes containing furnishings from redwood are obviously from California. And homes found in the Midwest are often filled with items made from hickory trees.

But, however romantic the setting appears, life in a one-room log cabin was less than ideal. Often a family of ten would occupy a single room, and I imagine that married couples had to make "certain arrangements" to continue on with both creating and raising a family. Further, bugs of all sorts were a real nightmare and historical literature is replete with sad stories of nightmarish ordeals. Frederick Law Olmsted, writing for the *New York Daily Times,* relates the following story. One man, overcome with the misery of invading insects spread corn shucks underneath his log cabin and lighted them on fire in hopes of smoking out the insects that were ruining his life. Tragically, his home caught fire, resulting in the deaths of his wife and family. In 1775, Philip Fithian wrote, "But o the fleas! Some mornings at some houses, I rise spotted and purple like a Person in the Measles!" And just to convince readers of how horrible such communities could become, Charles Dickens wrote his observations after viewing a few hundred log homes in Pennsylvania. He described them as "utterly forlorn and miserable in appearance." And after viewing more cabins in Virginia, he went on to describe these as "squalid to the last degree." And just to further convince people of the nature of early log cabin living, I must not fail to comment on our country's founder, George Washington. During the American Revolution, Washington's troops were housed in over a "thousand miserable log huts and over three thousand of his troops died of disease and privation." So, regardless of the romance associated with rustic living, it was hard and often brutal.

But rustic living is different today. Technology has made the lives

of all of us easier. Many rustic homes today are marvels of both technology and convenience. Consider this for a moment: many of the ultramodern rustic log homes are not true log homes. For the sake of quality, many rustic structures are "stick-built." That is, traditional construction techniques are used to "frame out" log homes. Wiring, plumbing and heating elements are incorporated into the frame walls. The walls are then insulated and covered with traditional materials. Then logs are split in half and applied to either the exterior and/or interior, thus resembling true log homes. True logs have an "R" (insulating) value of one "R" per inch. So an eight-inch log has an "R" value of only 8. True insulated and framed homes with log siding have an "R" value of up to 40, thus rendering them energy efficient.

All kinds of computerized amenities are also filling up rustic homes. And it's possible to sit in a mountaintop retreat and with the push of a few buttons have access to the entire world through the Internet.

But all things aside, there is, at the same time, a strong bond and spiritual connection to the past when either living in or building a log home. There is something about the feel and the shapes of the wood. There is something natural about the smells and textures of the logs. These are unspoken qualities that are not often mentioned, but as a writer and observer of human behavior, I know they are present. It's a feeling that calls to us all. That's why we have animals and plants in our homes and why we seek the solitude and peace of the woods. It's that very essence of nature, the place from which we all evolved, that calls to us. In truth, I can only speak for myself when I say that the warmth of the wood and the freedom inherent in the organic nature of trees calms my nerves and quiets my soul. But I believe that others feel as I do. I can see it in their eyes when they wander through a forest or a well-designed and constructed log home. Nature is part of all of us and it's foolish to resist.

I am being both truthful and a little biased when I say that today the Mecca of rustic home design and construction is Bozeman, Montana. Several major construction companies and individual artisans, as well as cutting-edge architects, live in the area. It seems that there is something in the water out there that brings out the best in rustic design and creations in humans. On Friday nights in the winter, the Ice Dogs, a semi-professional hockey team, play at the local ice arena. The parking lot is filled with trucks and vans with advertising logos for all sorts of log construction companies and design firms. Most of the trucks have racks in the back windows that hold guns and fishing rods. Many of the vans and trucks also have dogs patiently awaiting the return of their masters. In the arena, almost all of the more than two thousand spectators know each other. In general, they're a physically fit lot. Most have some sort of facial hair. They all wear baseball caps. Surprisingly, they seem to have all worked together at one time or another, for some company or architect. They share information. They are the men and women who build rustic homes. And they are a unique lot.

In truth, I've been in a hundred or so rustic homes in the Montana area. Every one of them is astounding. The people who both build and design these homes are artists in the truest sense. The architects, designers, and contractors encourage the hands-on builders to use their artistic capabilities to find solutions to problems. People are constantly encouraged to create. And from this environment magic happens! From the small guest cabins to the homes large enough

to sleep forty, the homes reflect a warmth and artistry that are the epitome of human artistic creativity.

Most of the people who own these homes have been very instrumental in their design. Many of the owners have also served as their own interior decorators. Almost all of the homes pictured within this book are second or third homes. Most owners have a very good "picture" in their minds of what they want the final product to be. And it's the architect's job to interpret the dreams of the client and bring such dreams to reality.

Architect Larry Pearson often tells stories with his homes. The homes he designs are family-oriented. He seeks to connect each home with the immediate environment. Clients encourage his creativity. They want his best.

He likes "experiences" within the setting. Homes, according to Larry, have to flow and have direction. They have to be intimate and inviting. They have to offer a succession of emotional experiences. Often the entryways to the homes of Larry Pearson are unassuming. One does not know what to expect when entering. A door opens and a small corridor leads visitors through a series of settings designed to enthrall and invite. The flat-stacked stone walls appear to be a part of the outside environment. The warm, rich, recycled timbers in the home invite touch. Occasionally, the old recycled boards on the floor "moan and creak" as I wander through a home. They seem to be speaking directly to me. The hand-hammered chandeliers throw subtle light on the setting and the roaring fire begs visitors to absorb its warmth. The timbers in the homes are usually harvested as "standing dead." The life has long gone from the trees and they have been recycled into a home. Once the bark has been removed, the logs are often finished with a brown wax that enhances the character of the wood. Often, long-gone bark beetles have left their trails on the surface, further enhancing the uniqueness of the wood. No attempt is made to hide or disguise the nature of the materials used in the setting. Pearson's homes are always a success.

Larry is a magical person. Every person I have met describes him as a "mad genius." And he is. He giggles quietly to himself and often breaks into an infectious smile and laughter. He's a big, burly kind of a guy. He wanders around his office shoeless and has time for questions from everyone. His door, unless he's in a serious meeting, is always open. Conversations between the two of us can go on for hours. When he inspects his many projects, he catches every detail. Art is his passion. The littlest things can thrill him. His homes reflect his genius.

His office is a bastion of creativity. I've probably spent a few hundred hours in his office over the years. Every one of the nearly thirty people in his office stays busy. Every one of them is incredibly competent at their job. The office is run by Jacque Spitler, who's been with Larry for nearly a decade. Jacque is the boss. You want her on your side. She does everything, from meeting new clients, managing complete construction projects, overseeing the staff, and providing interior design services for many of the homes, to keeping my own schedule intact. It appears that each of the architects and design people in Pearson's office is capable of doing all of the different tasks within their complex office. Sometimes they are designing doors and windows, then in the afternoon they may be master-planning a complete ski resort. It is an office filled with talented individuals who are encouraged to find creative solutions to problems at hand.

The office is also visited by many of the actual builders on a daily basis. They are constantly bringing in wood, color, and finish samples as well as examples of tile, shingles, stone and more types of materials than I can count. These are the meat-and-potatoes guys. They get the jobs done. Quality is the name of their game. They are artists in their own right and they, unfortunately, are often the unsung heroes of the building business. Homeowners never know their names, but their work stands as a monument to their individual creativity.

As I've been involved in the development of many homes around the country, I'm always shocked at how many decisions have to be made regarding the completion of a project. Thousands of details have to be considered and each one takes time. Art, they say— and to that I add the devil—is in the details. Colors have to blend. Homes have to have heat and water. Fireplaces have to draw flames. Basements and roofs must not leak. Windows and doors must work.

And so the evolution of the rustic home continues. The homes that appear in this book are unique. They are, in my humble opinion, national treasures. They speak to the ongoing evolution of rustic homes and stand as objects of art in themselves. But more than that, they are homes that bring families together in an atmosphere of warmth and beauty. The homes themselves inspire and bring out the best in humanity. They are the best!

ANDESITE RETREAT

Andesite Retreat

I HAD SEEN THIS HOME under construction over several different seasons. And, of course, when I finally decided to make photos of the home, it was winter. And, of course, I got stuck in the lengthy, downhill driveway in my four-wheel drive vehicle that was not supposed to ever get stuck in the snow.

Above: The massive front door, made from ancient hand-hewn timbers, was created by the craftsmen at Lohss Construction. Because of its weight, industrial-strength, ball-bearing hinges were required to correctly hang the door.

Right: The front hallway includes this massive formal staircase made from historic barn beams. Forged-iron balustrades serve as spokes for the staircase.

Opposite: An overview of the living and dining rooms. The hand-hewn beams used throughout the home came from a 150-year-old barn.

Preceding overleaf: A massive dry-stacked fireplace greets visitors as they enter the living room. Oversized upholstered chairs offer comfort to weary adventurers. The floor is recycled rough-cut pine. Antique skis from the 1940s rest on the fireplace mantel.

Opposite: The kitchen offers a center island complete with storage space on one side and ample space for Santa Fe chairs with leather tops on the other. The island top is pine. The countertop covering the sink area is dark granite. You can tell by the clock on the back wall that I made the photo at 2 p.m.! Drop fixtures covering the island are adorned with contemporary art glass shades.

Left: The dining room table has a two-inch-thick top made from old pine barn boards. The large side chairs are covered with a soft tapestry and the ceiling fixture is wrought iron.

An hour later I was fortunate enough to have several construction men (big guys!) from a project down the road help extricate me from a winter nightmare. Actually, the home would not have been a bad place to spend the winter, but I didn't think my wife and daughter, who were back at our home in Lake George, would approve. It was dark when I finally got down from the mountain.

Designed by architect Larry
Pearson and built by the creative
artists at Chris Lohss Construction,
the home serves as a vacation
residence for a young, active
family whose passions for skiing,
biking and hiking frequently
brings them to the mountains.
Offering views that would
intimidate even the bravest of
soaring eagles, the home sits on
a mountainside that is also home
to bears, elk, bighorn sheep
and moose. Described as a hand-
hewn post-and-beam structure,
the home comfortably sleeps
twenty-one people. An isolated
master wing allows for privacy
of the owners. The home also
consists of a guest bedroom,
bunkroom for the kids and their
many friends, kitchen, living
and dining rooms, and features
three fireplaces. An outdoor
hot tub, fireplace and two-car
garage finish the building.
Elizabeth Schultz was the
interior decorator for the project.

The master bedroom also
contains a fireplace, oversized leather armchairs
and soft textiles.

Opposite: The master
bathroom offers this cast-iron
soaking tub, plus views of
the forest and numerous
animals that wander by.

Top: A three-person sink occupies a corner of the bunkroom. The vanity is covered with vertical log application. Made from standing pine and recycled barn boards, the room is a perfect "get-away" for kids of all ages.

Above: A small half bathroom contains this rustic sink and stand. The sink was created from hammered copper. Locally quarried stones comprise the base.

BRAKOVICH CABIN

Brakovich Cabin

I HAD PASSED THE HOME several times through the years and had always admired both its form and location on the Big Wood River in Idaho. I had stood several times in full fly-fishing regalia in the front yard as I tied flies on my line in hopes of catching a few elusive brown trout. In time, my good friend rustic artist Doug Tedrow asked if I would like to see a wonderful riverside home full of great rustic furniture.

How could I refuse? Within the hour we are standing on the front porch of the home I had admired for years.

As a young girl, the owner of the home had spent significant time in the Adirondack Park of upstate New York. There she fell in love with the rustic forms of the many historical homes of that area. When it came time to build her own home, she asked architect Janet Jarvis of Ketchum, Idaho, to design a traditional Adirondack home that would blend into a Rocky Mountain setting. Contractor Frank Bashista, also of Ketchum, constructed the building. The owner of the home was responsible for the interior design.

The pair of stacked-log arm-chairs and rustic entertainment cabinet were created by rustic artist Doug Tedrow, of Wood River Rustics. Doug is an internationally known, award-winning artist from Ketchum. The ceiling structure was created from standing dead lodgepole pine trees.

Above: A further view of the chairs shows the detailed forms and coloring. The chairs also contain hidden compartments for storage. They rest on a hand-tied antique carpet.

Above: This western-style
pool table separates the
living room and kitchen
areas. The floors are covered
with recycled barn boards.
Radiant heat warms
the home.

The living room boasts
a fireplace with custom-made
fire screen. A moose head
hangs over the fireplace.
The coffee table was made
from recycled pine boards.

Above: The massive kitchen island is complete with a thick pine top. The floor is covered with fieldstone. The kitchen countertop is covered with sandstone. The lighting was made by Anvil Arts of Anaheim, California.

Left: This intricate mosaic island with ornate geometric pattern was created by Doug Tedrow. The mosaic work is created by splitting dried branches in half and then applying them to the surface of the furniture. The top of the island is also wood. Hickory bar stools serve as seating for the set.

Above, right, and opposite:
This majestic cupboard
was completed by Doug
Tedrow. Built in curvilinear
fashion to reside in the
circular dining room, the
cabinet serves as storage
space for collectibles and
eating paraphernalia.
The round table is also by
Tedrow. Contemporary
wicker chairs surround
the table.

Below: An upstairs bedroom offers a cozy fireplace and a king-size hickory bed from **Flat Rock Furniture, Inc.**

Opposite: The homeowners helped design this entryway console table that was constructed by Doug Tedrow. The legs and apron are lodgepole pine, while the top is alder.

Above left: The kids' bathroom offers this lengthy cast-iron sink to accommodate three individuals at one time. The top of the counter is pine.

Above center: This bathroom vanity and accompanying mirror were constructed by Doug Tedrow. The faucet and sink are nickel-plated.

Above right: The kids' bunkroom offers bunk beds, colorful textiles and its own antique pinball machine!

Left: This bathroom offers a view of the river while soaking one's aching muscles. The top of the vanity is covered with granite and the apron of the tub is covered with half-round lodgepole pine sticks.

THE CAPE

The Cape

"THE CAPE," the name given to this home by its owners, is not what one expects in the Rocky Mountains. Designed by Larry Pearson and influenced by the Cape homes of South Africa, the structure sits quietly on a calm prairie in one of the many bowls of the northern Rockies. As one turns into the driveway and travels through the tall grassland, the home slowly appears through the tall grasses and cottonwood trees that surround the complex.

The owners of the home had a clear vision of the structure they wanted. Actively involved in the design and decision-making process, they lived on another nearby section of the property and maintained a close connection throughout the design and construction phases. To ensure authenticity, Larry Pearson and the owner traveled to Capetown, South Africa, to study the intricacies of Cape Dutch architecture. They both educated and engrossed themselves in the art, culture and environment of the region. (I wish I could have gone along but lacked a formal invitation!) They were lucky enough to have a private tour of the Groote Schür (Great Grainery) in South Africa. This structure was the home of Cecil Rhodes, the prime minister of South Africa who earned his living through the DeBeers diamond mines. Arguably the most historic structure of the Cape Dutch styles, the building is the epitome of Royal Cape Dutch design.

The owners of The Cape are also active falconers who sought space for their birds and requested subtle architectural embellishments in the home for their passion in falcons and hunting. The final structure is a combination of both Royal and Country-style Dutch designs. The building, which contains two bedrooms, caretakers' quarters, library, dining and living rooms, is complete with massive porches designed for outdoor dining and entertaining.

The grounds of The Cape were designed to mimic South African landscaping. Surprisingly, the environment where the home presently sits closely resembles the varied terrain found in many regions of South Africa. To further embellish the immediate area, a small orchard was planted and alfalfa is harvested yearly. Stones were placed and shrubbery of all sorts was planted to enhance the grounds. Two ponds were carefully placed just off the back porch and massive cottonwood trees, often the resting spots for eagles, hawks and falcons, add a sense of wilderness to the property.

The feeling of the home is one of culture and sophistication. The rich colors and striking furnishings throughout distinguish this setting from other residences. Great care was taken to site the home correctly and to respect the indigenous environment. Meticulously constructed by the builders at Yellowstone Traditions, also of Bozeman, the home represents advanced artistic styling and craftsmanship. Greg Matthews served as the architectural project manager, and Ron Adams and Shaun Ryan, both of Yellowstone Traditions, served respectively as project manager and site supervisor. Rock artist Jamie Livingston served as mason for the project.

Entering the compound, I wondered what I was getting myself into. The skies had darkened throughout the day and the wind let itself be known. The tall grass appeared as rolling ocean waves as it followed the dictates of the gusts of air. In time, the rounded caps of the

multicurved parapet appeared over the tops of the flowing grasses. As we came closer to the structures, the complex appeared to have been in place for generations. The exteriors of the buildings were made of stucco and stone. No attempt had been made to alter the vegetation beyond the immediate borders of the home.

The house itself is both curious and inviting. What is this place doing in the Rocky Mountains? My first reaction was that is was Spanish/Moorish in design. I knocked with the lion's-head door knocker. Upon entering the home it was not in the least what I expected.

The grand back porch was designed for entertaining, eating and lounging. Stylized wicker furniture provides ample seating for afternoon lunches while overlooking indigenous prairies and ponds. (I will admit to spending a very relaxing few hours with friends as we enjoyed a great lunch and bottle of spirits!) The antique "planter's" chairs are also favorites for watching eagles hunt the nearby river.

Above: Just off the dining area is the music room, complete with player grand piano. The armoire on the back wall is made of stinkwood (it doesn't smell) and comes from South Africa. The covering on the piano bench is ostrich hide!

Antique furnishings bless the dining room as a leopard keeps careful watch from an overhead beam. Heavy mahogany corbels support the fireplace mantel on which resides naturally shed elk antlers and a pair of ibex candlesticks with ostrich egg shades. The rich plastered walls were carefully painted by color artist Jennifer Besson, of the Bitterroot Valley, Montana. The mantel, doors throughout the home and wood casework/paneling were masterfully created by Abbott Norris. The painting resting on the mantel is an early Dutch antique.

Opposite: The library is the most intimate room in the home. Both inviting and stimulating, a good book in front of a fireplace is all I need to be happy!

Three different views of the kitchen. The industrial stove is from the Aga Company. Made in England the stoves are noted for their efficiency and grand styling. The island top is honed black granite. The large painting over the stove was purchased in South Africa and was created by artist Vanbunben.

Above: The opposite end of the kitchen contains a dramatic built-in cupboard. Made of mahogany, the cabinet was constructed by Abbott Norris, of Norris Woodworking.

Right: A small bathroom off the kitchen is complete with a hammered-copper sink and faucets from the Fantasia Showroom in Bozeman. The ostrich painting was artfully created by C. Naylor. (I was extremely self-conscious when I made this photo—the bird seemed to be staring at me the entire time I was in the room!).

Opposite: A roaring outside fire on an enclosed back porch provides an ideal backdrop to watch the sun go down. The baskets and other artwork are from South Africa.

HOBBLE DIAMOND

Hobble Diamond

L IKE MANY OF THE HOMES I've visited through–
out the years, this one was very difficult to find.
Past fields of grasses where buffalo once roamed
and past towering cottonwood trees that held
the huge nests of birds of prey I drove. Deer and antelope were
more plentiful than I thought possible. Herds of such creatures
barely noticed us as we waved to them from our vehicle.

Above: This boot jack fence lines the entry to the compound and keeps the ranch cattle in their assigned space.

Right: A back-side view of the home includes lush lawns and wooded walkways to other buildings in the complex.

Preceding overleaf: Blending exquisitely with the surrounding environment, the home and guest house (on left) offer grand views of the prairies and extensive wildlife that visit the compound.

We stopped a few times to offer fresh grass to cows that were grazing by the miles of barbed wire but they "spooked" when we stopped the car. Apparently they were not fond of humans.

In time, we found a dirt road turn-off and followed the directions that had been given to us earlier in the day. In a few miles we were in the center of an extensive cattle ranch complex with barns, bunkhouses, silos, farm machinery of all sorts and several other structures whose purposes remain a mystery to me. Realizing that this setting was not the site of an architecturally significant home, we drove on. A vein of clear water, the Yellowstone River, appeared on our right and I longed to cast a few flies into the many pools that appeared before us. The river captured so much of my attention I nearly ran over a coyote that was chewing on a dead jackrabbit in the middle of the dirt road.

Soon the ground began to rise and rolling hills appeared before us. In the distance and tucked neatly into the foothills stood a structure that blended well with the surrounding colors of the prairie grasses. A boot jack fence lined the road that led us to the home.

The exterior consists of fir, lodgepole pine, cedar shingles and locally quarried Yellowstone River rocks. The extensive porches provide plenty of extra space for the kids on rainy days.

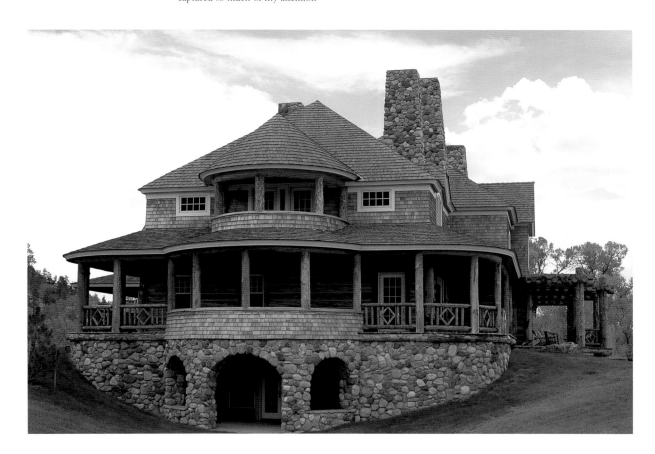

Designed by architect Kirk Michels of KMA, Inc., Livingston, Montana, the home and surrounding environment invited our curiosity. Grand in every way, the home was nothing less than spectacular. Like many conceptual homes, initially the size was to be small and intimate. But, like many projects, it grew dramatically as the owners requested further additions to allow for their three kids and the many friends who would be guests at the compound. Eventually the design was complete, and an appropriate site tucked in the hills and significantly back from the river was found.

The interior of the home is in excess of 10,000 square feet, and when the wraparound porches are added, the building encompasses 14,000 square feet of living space. Complete with six bedrooms, six full baths and three powder rooms, the home is a marvel of comfort, design, and ingenuity. KMA served as construction managers for the buildings, while Phillip Hooper and Sally Metcalf were the interior designers. As with many such projects, the homeowners were instrumental in the design of both the exterior and interiors of the homes on the property.

Opposite: The newel post for the staircase contains its root system and appears to be growing from the ground up! An advanced collection of cowboy memorabilia is displayed on the stairwell wall. An organic root bench sits below the staircase and allows for cowboys of all sorts a place to take off their boots.

Left: The entry hallway is complete with organic lodgepole pine banisters and railings. Knotty pine covers the walls in the entranceway. An antique Black Forest bear hall tree sits in a corner waiting for hats and other garments.

Above: A black bear overlooks the balcony on the second floor. A traditional tepee chandelier hangs from the ceiling. And a Y branch adds character to the balcony railing.

Opposite: An overview of the living room shows the seating area and ceiling log rafters. The floor is covered with rough-cut oak boards.

Left: The massive chimney and fireplace system was constructed from locally found Yellowstone River stones. A bison head hangs over the fireplace. The chandelier was designed by Philip Hooper and executed by Warren Welding of Livingston, Montana. Warren Welding also created the fireplace screens.

Below: A round antique continental table with claw feet offers display space for a variety of rustic collectibles. Along with cowboy hats, a ram's head and wild boar are displayed on the corner walls. A small Victorian chair sits neatly against a log wall.

Above: A gorgeous antique tall cabinet with original old paint and mouse holes lends character to the setting.

Right: A large wall in the living room is occupied by this sixteenth-century Dutch hunting scene.

Above: A small sitting room off the main living room offers guests comfortable upholstered furnishing in an intimate atmosphere.

Far left: A close-up of the fireplace mantel shows a cougar in a climbing position.

Left: A full wet bar with copper top and mosaic-inlay cabinet doors sits off the main living room.

Three views of the kitchen. The floor was created from rough-cut oak boards. The island was custom designed by architect Kirk Michels. Complete with stainless steel and an inlaid concrete top, the island is floating on casters that allow the piece to be moved for easy cleaning. The countertops are also concrete. The metal bar stools are complete with molded wooden seats. An industrial-strength stove allows for the preparation of meals by the private chef.

Two views of a bedroom show a fireplace featuring a log that the owner found on the property. Hides enhance the rusticity of the setting.

Below: Another of the six bedrooms in the home contains this delicate tree bed made by Diane Ross. White birch trees were used in its construction.

This stairway with massive logs as newel posts leads to the basement living area. The back wall contains a stone vanity complete with double bucket sinks! Antique cork screws neatly arranged in a frame hang on the wall over the sinks. The floor is sandstone.

The basement wine cellar has a complete dining area with an antique pine table, candle wall sconces made from red stag antlers, chairs with scrolled arms and an extraordinary sixteenth-century Dutch hunt scene.

Upper left: Another of the bathrooms offers a mosaic-inlay vanity with stone top, soaking tub, and deer skins on the floor.

Above: This basement shower room, with stone walls and floor, offers an overhead showerhead and a heavy stone sink.

Left: And when your muscles are aching after a hard day of "ropin' steers" or fly-fishing, you can wander into the massage room for a complete rubdown.

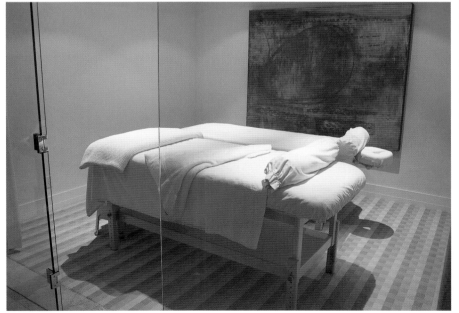

Right and opposite: Influenced by early national park designs, the bunkhouse features dramatic stone pillars, pointed log ends and a shake shingle roof.

The interior of the bunkhouse provides sleeping arrangements for many guests! Made of lodgepole pine, the bunks are finished with colorful textiles. The checkerboard fir floor was created by staining alternating sections dark and leaving the opposite sections natural.

The exterior of a second guest house on the property is finished with lodgepole pine and shake shingles.

The spiral staircase in the turret of the guest house was originally in place at a courthouse dating to 1935 in Townsend, Montana. The hub of the staircase was created from a 1908 tractor wheel.

Left: A small kitchen is sufficient to serve guests in the cabin. The island top was created from antique barn boards, and an antler chandelier provides subtle light for the area.

Above: These two French art deco leather armchairs allow visitors to relax in front of a roaring fire.

Far left: The kitchen in one of the remote rustic guest cabins offers a sink tucked into the side of a staircase.

Left: This massive antique armchair, which sits in a corner of the room, was created from the roots and burls of an old lodgepole pine tree.

LONE PEAK LOOKOUT

Lone Peak Lookout

ARGUABLY ONE OF THE MOST ELABORATE yet comfortable rustic structures ever created, this home began with a simple phone call and comment directed to architect Larry Pearson. The owner, a lover of antique structures, expressed concern about light in a historic building. An hour later, plans for the structure were set in motion.

Eighteen months later, the owners walked into their 10,300-square-foot, world-class rustic home! At face value it seems almost impossible that a home of this magnitude could be completed in such a short time. But a highly coordinated residential construction team put forth enormous effort and finished the structure in time for the family to enjoy the Christmas holidays in it!

The owners of the home were very involved in the conception and design of the building. The family includes four kids and numerous extended relatives. Ultimately, the home evolved to include six bedrooms, eight bathrooms, a living and dining room, office, workout room, entertainment room, kitchen, three-car garage, extensive porches with hot tub, balconies with sitting rooms, six fireplaces and a few other rooms to boot!

Several of the rooms have heights that measure twenty-five feet from floor to ceiling. It is a very cool place.

The home was constructed by the talented folks at OSM Builders in Bozeman, Montana. At any given time, between forty and fifty-five craftsmen were on-site, diligently working on the project. Visiting the site several times during its construction, I was always amazed at the number of people working side by side on what appeared to be completely different facets of the home. And then one day it all fell into place.

OSM Builders (aka On-Site-Management) have been around since the late 1970s. With significant homes completed over the years, the company had the experience to carefully coordinate and orchestrate many subcontractors, craftsmen, and suppliers to create a structure that stands out for its design and craftsmanship.

The homesite sits at about 9,000 feet above sea level. The area surrounding the home is a zone four seismic fault region. The foundation, masterfully created and engineered by Ed Matos of Bridger Engineering, rests safely and securely in solid andesite stone. It took a month longer than expected to jackhammer the rocks and set the foundation. Because of serious snow at that elevation, the building had to support 200 pounds of snow load per square foot. Once the foundation was in, a steel substructure was erected that looked like nothing less than the framed skeleton of a skyscraper. One hundred tons of steel—actually red iron—was used in the substructure. (An interesting note: on the second-floor balcony doorway, the overhead beam was significantly too low to allow for comfortable passage through the walkway. A section had to be cut, re-welded and then covered with an old barn post to disguise the metal beam.)

The stonework was far more complicated than initially expected, and three crews from different masonry firms were brought in to complete the rock work for the home. Guy Fairchild, Angel Sandoval and Phil Cox each provided crews to complete the extensive stonework. Known locally as Harlow stone, the materials came from the Harlowton Quarry in Montana. (As an aside, the first time I photographed the home, we started a fire in the kitchen fireplace. Tragically, the flue was closed [it wasn't my fault!] and the home quickly filled with smoke. Moments later, the fire department showed up and proceeded to lambaste us for our incompetence and irresponsibility.)

Right: Arguably the greatest rustic door ever created, this masterpiece rests on hand-made ball-bearing hinges. The hardware was hand-forged by Will Wilkins.

Opposite: The hallway off the main entrance has twenty-five-foot ceilings. Handmade, old-world rustic cabinets house warm coats and all kinds of other stuff.

The formal staircase, as the architect refers to it, is just off the main entrance. The ancient timbers radiate warmth and character. A twig-mosaic door to a downstairs bathroom is also seen.

The trees for the porches offer interesting tales as well. The steel beams for the back porch were completely wrapped by huge standing dead cedar trees that were acquired in Canada specifically for this project. The butts of many of the trees were in excess of sixty inches across. The trees were split in half, hollowed out and then wrapped around the beams to obscure their presence. Because some of the bark began to fall from the trees, new bark had to be applied with nails and glue. Steve Simpson and Eric Nellis were the log artists who completed the porch and much of the remaining log work in the home. The project required 6,500 linear feet of logs plus 140,000 board feet of dimensional lumber.

Arguably the most interesting piece of reclaimed wood was used as the mantels for both the upstairs and downstairs fireplaces. Found at the bottom of the St. Lawrence Seaway, a solid oak 21" x 22" x 22' bridge piling was rescued from where it had sat underwater for almost two hundred years. Weighing more then 7,000 pounds, the beam was transported via flatbed truck to its final location in the Rocky Mountains. Huge cranes were used to set the mantels in place.

Another area of interest is the old section of the home. OSM Builders, eight years earlier, had acquired an extraordinary historical structure made of notched logs from British Columbia. The materials from this structure, referred to as the BC stack, were used to create the master wing of the home. The stairway in the master wing proved to be a challenge as well. A forty-foot center stair column had to be dropped into the building by crane, and onto that the stairs and various landings were attached. Spencer Archer of OSM oversaw the completion of the staircase.

Top left: A view of the kitchen fireplace. The cabinets were made from antique barn boards. If you look closely, you'll see smoke from the fireplace near the ceiling of the room. A half hour before the photo was made, the room was filled with smoke, necessitating a visit by very irate firemen. We forgot to open the flue before we lit the fire!

Below left: A view of the kitchen includes an industrial range. The handmade range hood was created by Will Wilkins. The countertops are St. Andrews Limestone.

Below right: The kitchen cabinets were created in the workshops of OSM. Radiant heat warms the floor.

Opposite: View of the kitchen shows the green tiles that outline the cooking area. Wrought-iron chairs with wooden plank seats serve as seating around the island.

The coolest and most original room of the house, at least to my taste, is the second-floor bunkroom. Containing wildly organic materials, the room was masterfully completed by rustic artists Gabe Williams and Shawn Gadberry of OSM. The materials, regarded mostly as scraps, were acquired during hundreds of hours wandering the local mountains. The room took about a month to complete. Architect Larry Pearson required that the builders throw away their tape measurers and rulers and build the beds in organic fashion. Once completed, the beds were finished with wipe-on polyurethane and wax.

Right: A close-up view of the dining room set. Mirror frame above the mantel is made from the antlers of mule deer.

Opposite: An ornate antler mirror sits above the mantel. The massive dining room table was created from ancient barn boards in the workshops of OSM. The antique walnut chairs are in late Mission style and were reupholstered in suede. The two large armchairs were custom made to complement the side chairs. The chandelier that holds eighteen candles was made by Will Wilkins.

The lighting in the home is also unique. Will Wilkins of Firesong Forge completed the huge chandeliers and sconces, as well as much of the door hardware and other iron accessories. Joe Holley of Gansevoort, New York, completed many of the smaller sconces and other hardware. Initially, the living room chandeliers were designed to be lit with candles. It eventually became clear that it's far easier to throw on an electrical switch than to lower the chandeliers and light candles. The chandeliers were then wired for electricity.

All in all, the entire project was completed on time. The owners and architect encouraged creativity in all of the craftspeople involved. And it has been mentioned by several people that the most challenging thing about the project was the communication amongst the many people it took to complete the project. And if I may say so, they did an absolutely grand job!

A cutaway of the entrance to the old section, which houses the master bedroom, office and baths. A massive hand-hewn timber adds drama to the setting.

On a personal note, I photographed the home on four different occasions. The most difficult aspect of my job was photographing the exteriors. On two separate occasions I had to wander some hundred yards from the home to make photos of the entire house. At face value this is no big deal. But with five feet of snow on the ground, zero degrees, forty MPH winds, at 9,000 feet above sea level and lugging fifty pounds of photographic gear, it was no fun! In truth, the exterior photos nearly put me into cardiac arrest. But if it had happened right there, it was truly not a bad place to step into the great beyond!

Along these same thoughts, this and many of the other homes I photographed for this book are absolute monuments to the creativity of all humanity. In truth, I could have easily stayed in this one home and made many more photos.

The organic staircase in the old section of the house is secured by a huge center stair column that had to be installed using a crane.

Above: A section of the second-floor hallway offers four massive, four-foot cylinder chandeliers lined with amber mica. The chandeliers were designed by Larry Pearson and executed by Will Wilkins.

Left: A view of the second-floor balcony shows the ceiling beams and a partial view of a dormer.

Opposite: Numerous ancient standing dead logs add strength to a very complicated roof system. This is a view of the second-floor balcony, which contains numerous nooks and crannies for bookshelves and hiding places. The doorway at the far end of the balcony was originally built too low. To the chagrin of the builders, a section of an I-beam needed to be cut and raised to accommodate the passage of humans to adjoining rooms.

Three views of the
second-floor bunkroom.
Made of a combination of
jack pine and lodgepole
pine tree scraps, the
beds were created by
Gabe Williams and
Shawn Gadberry of OSM.
An original Ganado
Navajo throw rug hangs
on the wall.

Above: This nook on the second-floor balcony offers two red modified Chesterfield sofas.

Right and opposite: A view of the living room shows the massive circular chandeliers. Originally designed to hold just candles, the fixtures were electrified once someone realized that en enormous effort would be needed to light the room with just candles.

Above: In a corner off
the living room sits this set
of four antique chairs.
The antique round table is
made of cedro wood. An
antique Ganado Navajo
carpet rests on the old pine
board floor. The flooring
is secured with rose-
head nails.

Above: A series of sconces handmade by Will Wilkins outlines the exterior of the home.

Above center: The master bedroom is complete with a king-sized bed and a fireplace. The couch at the foot of the bed is Art Deco and covered in leather.

Above right: A small sitting room off the master bedroom serves as an office for the owner. An original Gustav Stickley desk and armchair allow the owner to catch up on business.

Right: The master bathroom is complete with handmade cabinets that are covered with Calcutta Luna marble, imported from Italy. An original Navajo rug covers the floor.

Two views of the downstairs recreation room show a grand fireplace and an antique Monterey game table with matching chairs. The set is from the mid-1930s. The massive mantel over the fireplace was reclaimed from the bottom of the St. Lawrence Seaway. The solid oak beam weighed more than 7,000 pounds and was 22 feet long when found.

MONTANA LALU

Montana
Lalu

PERHAPS THE MOST ADVANCED INTERPRETATION of a rustic home, this structure was designed by Larry Pearson for an enthusiastic couple from Texas. A discriminating couple with two young children, they wanted a different type of ski home. They wanted no logs and they wanted the home to reflect their lifestyle and contemporary values.

The home was constructed by Chris Lohss. Interior designer extraordinaire Carol Hammil, of Dallas, was the interior decorator for the project.

I must admit that the house was not at all what I expected. From the outside, it appeared fairly innocuous and unassuming. As with many of the other homes in this book, I had watched its development and was excited to see the interior once the project was completed. When I finally drove down the driveway to see and photograph the home with Queen Jacque Spitler (who acted as my photo stylist that day), there was six feet of snow on the ground.

Contemporary and modern in every way, the home was more in the style of George Jetson than Abe Lincoln. But it works and it works well!

Preceding overleaf, left: This complete kitchen component was created by the German firm of Bulthaup. The iron barstools in the Berttola style are by Knoll.

Preceding overleaf, right: This industrial-strength staircase is complete with I-beams and exposed metal caging. The steps are fir slabs.

Right: This ebonized dining table is complete with glass inlay top.

Left top and bottom: The living room sofas are by the Italian firm Minotti. The red "Bird" chairs are by Knoll. The Indian jars on the fireplace mantel are antique. The coffee table is by the Italian firm Casa Armani.

Below: The downstairs bath offers a full soaking tub and direct views of the ski slope.

Top left: Referred to as the "Zen" bed, this oriental platform bed was designed by Carol Hammil and hand-crafted by Steve Davenport of Bozeman. The floors throughout the entire building are concrete.

Top right and below: The master bedroom also offers this soaking tub and window bench.

Left: The downstairs play-room is complete with a wraparound sectional sofa by Ligne Roset of Italy. The coffee table is by Casa Armani.

Below: This downstairs bedroom offers a modern bed with lime-green bed coverings.

MOUNTAIN GUEST

Mountain Guest

ARCHITECT LARRY PEARSON was approached by a discriminating client couple who owned property at a very high elevation in the Rocky Mountains. Outdoor enthusiasts, they wanted first a small cabin for guests and then a much larger home for themselves on the property. Completed in 2005, the guest home is a model of charm, warmth, intimacy, uniqueness and quality.

Over the course of the past few years, I've had the opportunity to visit the cabin at various stages of its completion. At nine thousand feet above sea level, I can assure readers that a visit to the home is no easy feat for us aging East Coasters.

Opposite and above: A wintertime view shows the dramatic scenes offered by the setting. It is not uncommon for more than fifteen feet of snow to acquire in the area.

The home has dramatic architectural lines. The vertical stones on top of the chimney are commonly referred to as a "soldiers course."

Preceding overleaf: The notched antique beams were part of the old Lewis Homestead. This building became part of the new structure at the cabin.

Above: A detail section of the porch railing shows the creative use of standing dead materials.

Right: The front door was also made from recycled materials gathered from the Lewis Homestead. The front entryway floor is made of Mojave quartzite sandstone.

Opposite: The front hallway features benches made from recycled flooring. Heated pipes under the flooring, referred to as radiant heating, warm the home.

But from my perspective (and I am extremely biased), here's the truth about the cabin: its small size (about fifteen hundred square feet), its design (both architecturally and the interior decor), its use of recycled materials, the quality of construction and its views make the home stunning beyond belief. Small rooms and low ceilings foster intimacy. Although the living room has a partial vaulted ceiling, the tie logs and height of the custom chandelier require users to remain focused on things in the immediate environment.

Custom-made by the creative folks at Lohss Construction, the home comes in two sections. The master bedroom is actually a recycled cabin that was found, dismantled and reassembled. Called the Lewis Homestead, the original home was about 150 years old. The remaining part of the new home was made of locally found stone and ancient timbers. The house is small, containing two bedrooms, a living/dining room, a small kitchen, two baths, two small loft areas and a small section of hallways. The stonework was created by Angel Sandoval of Sandoval Masonry. The owners provided much of the interior furnishings and artwork.

Above: Large Spanish-style chairs surround the dining room table. The chairs and couch were upholstered with bold Turkish kilim material. The interior of the room (and much of the remainder of the home) was finished with half-round standing dead pine logs. The floors are covered with rough-cut recycled pine boards. The ladder to the loft area was made from lodgepole pine.

Right: The massive ten-light chandelier was handmade by blacksmith artist Joe Holley, of upstate New York. The fireplace is the creation of Angel Sandoval.

Opposite: Another overview of the living room reveals paintings and other artistic accessories.

Opposite: An ornate Heartland stove rests in the small kitchen. The kitchen cabinets were made from rough-cut pine and the countertop is of black granite.

Left: The open-shelf pantry that leads to the kitchen is complete with a matching Heartland refrigerator.

Above: A lengthy desk/vanity occupies a small hallway that leads to the master bedroom. The countertop is actually recycled floor boards from the original Lewis Homestead. The rough edge on the countertop is referred to as either a wained or a hewn edge.

Above: An iron bed frame is enhanced with a padded leather inset. The bright red colors of the bedding add life to the setting.

Right: The master bedroom contains an iron bed complete with colorful textiles.

The bathroom ceiling contains this intricate mosaic work in geometric design. Round lodgepole pine branches are cut in half and applied.

Below: The large Kohler "Vintage" tub, which weighed more than seven hundred pounds, proved to be a challenge to install.

OLD ROOT CELLAR

The
Old Root
Cellar

WE HAD DRIVEN MORE THAN AN HOUR and were wondering where exactly we were. But the scenery softened our nerves and the deer, antelope, and occasional elk were a pleasure to behold. Finally, beside an old barbed-wire fence, we found a keypad that, once the correct code was entered, opened a steel gate.

Onto a dirt road we drove. Fields
of tall golden grasses swayed with
the winds and huge old cottonwood trees distinguished themselves with a majestic display of
golden fall colors. In time, we
approached an ancient steel
bridge that appeared to be on the
verge of collapse. Throwing cau-
tion to the wind, I inched our
rental vehicle onto the structure
and held my breath as it moaned
and groaned while we made our
way across the river below.
Gradually, the road narrowed
until it nearly disappeared. Then,
in a stand of old cottonwoods,
three richly decorated tepees
appeared. I decided against seeing
if anyone was home.

This page and preceding
overleaf: Driving down a long
dirt goat path, one had to
drive slowly to avoid hitting
the many deer that grazed
close to the road. The small
home was originally a root
cellar that had been magi-
cally transformed into an
exceptional rustic retreat
complete with sod roof and
a bison skull adorning the
front lawn.

Without fanfare, an unassuming form that resembled an old mining shack slowly appeared. I had been told that an architecturally significant home was on the property and that I would have no problem finding the structure. But as I looked around, nothing of major consequence was evident. So, with hope dwindling, I peeked in the windows of an old root cellar. I was not in the least disappointed in what I saw.

Designed by architect James Morton, who tragically passed away before the completion of the project, the Old Root Cellar, as it has been affectionately named, was constructed by the exceptionally talented people at Yellowstone Traditions, of Bozeman. Patti Snyder of the Snyder Design Group, Billings, Montana, served as interior decorator for the project. The Old Root Cellar currently serves as a guest home, until the main building, presently under design, is completed.

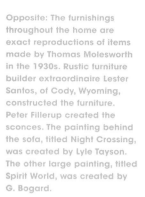

Opposite: The furnishings throughout the home are exact reproductions of items made by Thomas Molesworth in the 1930s. Rustic furniture builder extraordinaire Lester Santos, of Cody, Wyoming, constructed the furniture. Peter Fillerup created the sconces. The painting behind the sofa, titled Night Crossing, was created by Lyle Tayson. The other large painting, titled Spirit World, was created by G. Bogard.

Top left: A small built-in kitchen is adequate for guests and visitors. An antique Ganado Navajo carpet covers the floor.

Top right: The kitchen set was created by the Old Hickory Furniture Company in the 1930s. The chandelier is by Peter Fillerup.

Bottom left: The bed was created by Lester Santos. The recycled beams and timber used throughout the home were acquired from an old Idaho coal-mining shaft.

Bottom right: The large cabinet and western armchair were constructed by Lester Santos. The paintings on the cabinet doors are by George Dabich. The chandelier is by Peter Fillerup. The large painting, titled Horse Thief, was painted by E. W. Deming. Another bright Navajo carpet covers the floor. The building is warmed by radiant heat. The floor is made from Idaho quartzite stone.

PIONEER LOOKOUT LODGE

Pioneer Lookout Lodge

O VERLOOKING A MASSIVE VALLEY and nestled neatly into a mountainside rests this rustic home. Constructed by Chris Lohss and designed by Larry Pearson, the home is the delight of its owners. Gallatin Valley Furniture of Bozeman, Montana, was the interior decorator.

Preceding overleafs: These views of the home show the varying levels of the building. Complete with dormers, large overhangs and chimneys, the home blends well into the countryside. Eight feet of snow on the ground is pretty common here, so the roof is designed to accommodate heavy snow loads. The ski slopes are right out the cabin's back door.

Opposite: An overview of the living room shows oversized wing chairs and leather couches. The floor is covered with old barn boards. Radiant heat warms the home. Often described as the soul of the home, this massive fireplace invites owners and guests to cozy up and relax.

Left: The downstairs recreation area features a full wet bar surrounded by hickory barstools complete with thick leather seats. The countertop is a three-inch-thick piece of slab pine. Lighting in this area is classic Arts and Crafts copper chandeliers with amber mica.

Conceived as a mountain family retreat, the home maintains strong lines that are enhanced by wraparound porches. Spacious and comfortable, the home is complete with fireplaces, bunk-rooms and game rooms. It also offers protected breezeways and entryways.

The exterior of the home is made interesting by both vertical and horizontal log placement, as well as significant rock work. The roofing is shake shingles.

The kitchen island is sided with wainscoting. The top of the island is dark granite. The refrigerator is Jenn-Air. The floor is covered with soapstone tiles. Hickory barstools surround the island. An Arts and Crafts cylinder chandelier lights the kitchen area. The cabinetry was crafted by Chris Kurowski.

Opposite: The dining room offers this stylish, modern set of eight side chairs and two armchairs. Antique terra-cotta tiles cover the dining room floor.

Above: A view of the downstairs bedroom shows the staircase, made of standing dead lodge-pole pine. Built-in cabinets under the window seat serve as storage space.

The bedroom offers Arts and Crafts sconces on either side of the bed, as well as an iron ceiling chandelier with hide shades.

Like many advanced, energy-efficient rustic homes today, the structure was stick built and then covered with half-round logs, thus rendering the home "rustic" in every way.

Constructed in this fashion, all wiring, plumbing and insulation are easily installed and completely hidden from view. An extensive fire suppression system also remains hidden in the logs.

Above: Another downstairs bedroom is complete with a queen-sized bed covered with bright red comforter.

Left: An upstairs bunkroom is fitted with massive bunk beds for the kids.

Below: Off the bunkroom is this large alcove, which is a nice retreat for those who want to get away from it all and just read for a while.

RANCHO RELAXO

Rancho Relaxo

O N THE SHORES of a major river in the Montana Rockies sits this rustic home. A stone's throw from the water, the grounds are visited daily by more deer than I had ever seen at one time. Elk and moose also stop by and an occasional bear wanders right past the porch. Wolves and coyotes also pay occasional visits. With dramatic mountains in the background, this home is perfectly named!

As a frequent visitor to the area, I had floated by here several times while fly-fishing before I realized the home was designed by Larry Pearson.

The owners of this home spent significant time in Montana looking for a vacation house that would meet their needs. One day while in the Ennis area, they saw a building under construction that was exactly what they were looking for. The architect for that structure was Larry Pearson. They contacted Pearson and had him design their home.

Rancho Relaxo (I love the name) was constructed by Bill Keshishian of Elephant Builders. Shelby Rose was architectural project manager. Built on what was described as a flood plain, during a recent high water flood the home stood on dry solid ground! Seeking minimum environmental impact, no trees were removed to construct the home or nearby barn. The owners were actively involved in the design and construction and the completion of the building went smoothly.

Energy-efficient rustic homes today are actually "stick built." It is infinitely easier to run electricity, plumbing and insulation through the walls of a stick-built home than through solid logs. And a traditionally built home has far greater insulation capabilities than a true log home, for reasons explained earlier.

Rancho Relaxo was stick built and then sided with half-round slabs from worm-killed, dead standing trees. The logs retain all of their natural character, and no finish or preservatives are applied to them once they are set in place. The natural aging and weathering of such logs greatly adds to the character of the building. Steve Diekman was the log wizard who applied the siding to the home.

The Rancho also has what appears to be an old rusty roof. This is actually a high-tech steel roof created from what is called "cold rolled" steel. A very thin outer layer of the roof quickly rusts when exposed to the elements. Underneath the rust is another thick layer of steel designed to withstand many years of harsh weather. A rusted roof enhances the charm of the building. In this particular home, river rocks were used to create the chimney. Dan Hanson was the mason on this project.

A reproduction Tiffany-style chandelier (affectionately called the "disco ball") lights the entryway to the living room. The floor and built-in bookcases were made from recycled pine.

Windsor chairs surrounding a country pine table provide ample seating for dinners. Steve Handelman of Santa Barbara completed the iron chandeliers in the dining room and elsewhere throughout the home.

Opposite: The fireplaces were made from locally found river rocks. The process of finding and acquiring the correct stones for the fireplaces took four months.

Above: The countertop in the kitchen is a three-inch slab of pine. The wrought-iron bar stools are complete with embossed leather tops.

Right: The kitchen is complete with an industrial Viking stove. The kitchen island countertop is granite.

Opposite: An upstairs hallway offers a secluded corner for a comfortable reading chair.

Opposite: The centerpiece of the master bedroom is an iron bed covered with an antique patchwork quilt. Shelves lining the end wall make the room highly functional as well.

Left: Two sets of bunk beds were constructed from dead pine trees for the upstairs bunkroom. The beds are covered with down comforters and animal skins.

Lower left: Recycled boards were utilized to frame the doorways. The bathroom countertop is granite and the faucets are Rohl Country.

Right: An old galvanized tub was used as a sink in the main bathroom. The countertop is a slab of thick pine

THE ROOKERY

The Rookery

I ARRIVED VERY LATE AT NIGHT. I had spent more than thirty hours stuck in various airports due to cancelled flights because of heavy fog. I was exhausted. I said very little before I passed out. Around six a.m. I could hear the honking of geese. I opened the door and wandered into the darkness. Over the lake hung a vibrant thumb-nail moon and over that floated Venus.

Preceding overleafs:
More than a hundred yards of
cattails cover the front yard
before one gets to water. The
home is called the Rookery
because of the enormous
amount of birdlife that
occupies the area in the
warm months.

Right: A side view showing
the casual walkway to the
front door.

Opposite: The exterior of the
main home is covered with
recycled pine boards.
The peeling paint adds
character. The roof is
covered with asphalt
composite shingles.

Other stars dazzled me. I could hear deer as they crashed through the brush. The geese honked louder as the deer made their way through the dried cattails.

The birth of dawn on that day brought purple skies. Fog rolled in and out like cars in a gas station. Soon the sun popped out, only to disappear again behind thick layers of airborne moisture. Shortly, I returned to my bed, leaving the windows wide open, and snoozed for another half hour. I was more relaxed than I had been in quite a while.

Designed by Larry Pearson as a family hideaway and constructed by Tom Lennoch, the home was originally intended to be smaller. But like many projects, and with the realization that many friends would come calling once they learned about the lake house, the home quickly expanded to include bunkrooms and an attached guest cabin. Rustic in spirit, the home has become the absolute delight of the owner and his family.

The owner envisioned a vacation home that presented the influences of both the East and West. But it was designed with a story in mind and evolved to look more like a Cape Cod summer home than a western ranch.

Many homes in the early years included add-ons. As families grew, additions were tacked onto the main house. The Rookery was built to convey this same feeling. The main house was sided with recycled shiplap pine complete with old, peeling white paint. The guest quarters were completed with shake shingles stained green.

Further, most vacation homes historically and today have been furnished with unused furnishings from the owner's permanent home. Vacation homes are receptacles of heritage. It is a style that I affectionately refer to as "Camp Hand-Me-Downs." The owner wanted this home to have that same presence. So a wide variety of furnishings styles, all sorts of bric-a-brac as well as collectibles and memorabilia were added to the home. Comfort, casualness, and fun were the main guidelines for the creation of this home.

Opposite: Visitors enter through a year-round heated breezeway. Created from ancient recycled materials, exposed 2 x 4s created an authentic cabin look. This section of the home is filled with collectibles of all sorts, antique hickory furniture, vintage canoe paddles, old signs and snowshoes. An original Gustav Stickley even-arm settle provides a place for visitors to watch the sunsets. The large fireplace, created from Montana moss rock, was constructed by Angel Sandoval. Radiant heat warms the room on cold nights.

Left: At the top of the stairs, separating the living room and kitchen, sits this set of antique Monterey dining room furniture.

Opposite: The living room contains a variety of vintage Arts and Crafts chairs and other furnishings. The round glass balls on the shelf are Oriental fishing buoys.

Left: In the corner of the game room sits this gorgeous antique Scandinavian cupboard wearing old blue paint.

Above: Another large antique cupboard from Scandinavia provides storage space for the owner. Much of the main house is heated by radiators. The fir floor throughout the main house was reclaimed from a schoolhouse gymnasium built in the 1920s in Leesburg, Oregon.

Right: Off the dining room is the game room. An original Gustav Stickley table and vintage 1930s Old Hickory chairs are host to visitors playing all sorts of table games.

Below: A downstairs gathering room offers space for informal activities and chatting. A vintage Old Hickory coffee table sits in the middle of the room. A log chair and settee (which weigh a ton and are a nightmare to move), and other armchairs offer sufficient seating.

Opposite: The kitchen is complete with wainscoted cupboards and island. Lodgepole pine trees with intact roots were used for the corners of the island. The cupboards were painted to add light to the room. The chandelier with four hanging Edison bulbs was created by Etak Electric from a piece of driftwood found on the shores of the lake. The countertops for the island sink area were constructed from Honduras mahogany.

Above: A variety of colored objects, including food cans, dinnerware, flowers, fruits and vegetables, add life to the setting. The stove is set into the island countertop. My breakfast is cooking in the frying pan and steam rising from the tea kettle is ready for morning coffee.

View of the kitchen and living room of the guest quarters. A 1950s chrome set serves as a dining table and chairs. Comfortable rattan furniture brings a sense of ease to the setting.

Left: The master bedroom offers this king-sized bed with warm comforters for cold nights.

Above: A rectangular two-faucet sink rests in the bathroom. Driftwood was used for railings in the home.

Far left: The downstairs bunkroom sleeps four. Made from dimensional wood, the bunks have numerous drawers at the bottom for storage space.

Left: Brightly colored checkerboard quilts cover the beds in one of the kids' rooms.

ROOT RANCH

Root Ranch

FROM MY HOME in Lake George, New York, I drove to Albany to catch an early morning flight. From Albany I flew first to Detroit and then to Seattle, where I had a five-hour wait for the next flight to Eugene, Oregon. From there I boarded another small plane and finally landed in Medford, Oregon. Of course, my luggage was lost in transit.

It was now about 8 p.m. West Coast time. I found a hotel room and then returned to the airport late in the night to retrieve my luggage. I parked my rental vehicle in front of the terminal. Other than a few ticket agents, no one was around. I was quite happy to see my luggage sitting by the counter not more than twenty feet from me. As I approached my bags, a booming voice loomed loud in my ears.

"Sir, you cannot leave your vehicle unattended."

"But I just need to pick up my bags which are right there."

A variety of exterior photos of the home indicate the hands-on, old-world feel of the building, with vertical rather than horizontal placement of logs. The home sits quietly on the shores of a small pond. A few feet beyond the pond exist numerous cold springs, which the owners have lovingly restored and restocked with monster trout. (I didn't dare ask if I could fish either the streams or pond.)

"Sir, move you vehicle immediately or I'll issue you a ticket."

"Ma'am, I'll be right there."

"Sir, move your car immediately or I'll call the sheriff."

The baggage handler said he would bring my bags to the vehicle, but to no avail; the sheriff, with an oversized gun on her hip, suddenly appeared.

"Sir, move your vehicle now."

"I'm just getting my bags," I said assertively.

Far left: Innovative and dramatic, the radial form of the central fireplace is evident throughout the gathering spaces of the home. The floor in the lower gathering room is covered with Oregon flagstone. Radiant heat warms the home. Recycled vintage barn beams serve as spokes radiating from the top of the fireplace. The large stones at the base of the fireplace, called sittings stones, are tumbled granite.

Left: Another view of the central fireplace. The cylinder chandeliers with mica inserts were acquired in Argentina. The exterior walls (behind and to the left of the fireplace) were created from recycled foundation sandstones acquired from a Fort Klamath, Oregon, building.

"Sir, get in your vehicle now; move your car or you'll be placed under arrest."

A crowd had now gathered and was anxiously awaiting my next move. I moved the car. At that moment, I hated everything and everybody.

The following morning, I realized I had no idea where the home was or how to get there. I was fortunate to have reached the architect's office and they promised to immediately fax directions. An hour later and after three tries to get the fax machine to work, I finally had directions emailed to someone off-site and then emailed back to the hotel office and printed out.

From there I started driving. Within half an hour, I was sitting in a complete fog whiteout. I called the homeowner from my cell phone and she politely gave me further directions. I drove the next fifty miles at ten miles per hour. Finally, I gave up and again called the homeowner.

"Where are you?"

"I don't know."

"What do you see out your window?"

"White."

"How about in back or on the sides?"

"Just white." In truth, I could not see ten feet in any direction of the car.

"I'll come and get you," the owner mercifully said. Half an hour later, I saw the headlights of a car. I had been rescued! I followed the owner back to the home.

All of my anger and anxiety melted away when I first saw the house. In absolutely the middle of nowhere, the home blended perfectly with the immediate environment.

The project was first designed by Larry Pearson on the back of a napkin at Melitas Café in Chiloquin, Oregon. The napkin has, unfortunately, disappeared and an enormous amount of searching by many people has failed to produce the original "doodle" of the project. Initially conceived in 1998, the project underwent numerous revisions and was completed in the spring

Opposite: A further view of the central fireplace.

Left: This alcove offers comfortable leather chairs. The walls are covered with recycled redwood.

Above: A collection of brightly colored vegetables, Depression glass ware and painted bowls sits on top of this farm table, which retains its old mustard-color paint.

Right: The dining room table and chairs were designed by Larry Pearson and Ricardo Paz of the Arte Étnico Argentino in Argentina. Pearson is well known for his support of native groups. The table was made of just three pieces of algarrobo wood running the full length of the table; it's rare to find pieces that long. The chairs are made from mature Argentinian woods with leather-hide woven seats. The iron chandelier, also acquired in Argentina, holds eighteen candles. The antique wall rugs are also from Arte Étnico Argentino.

Opposite: Another view of the dining room set and chandelier.

Opposite: The kitchen island offers an inset range and working sink. The top section of the island is covered with copper, while the lower section is covered with black granite. The base of the island and other cabinets in the kitchen were created from recycled barn boards.

Left: The bar stools are also from the Arte Étnico Argentino company in Argentina. The range hood was created from hammered copper.

Above: A Heartland reproduction stove sits in the kitchen.

of 2006. The owners of the home, an international couple, wanted their new residence to be both discrete and innocuous. They wanted it to have historic values. They wanted it to blend perfectly with the vast landscape on which the home was to rest. It had to be low to the ground and it had to be "handmade."

Eventually the design took on both a radial form and linear drama. The home (I've only seen it covered with snow, mind you) looks like it has always been there. Constructed by John Simpson, the project contains a variety of recycled materials. Adam Britt served as project manager. The rock for the walls, floors and fireplaces came from three different sources. Old barn boards and standing dead lodge-pole pine trees were also used within the building. Bill Peace of Peace Design acted as interior designer and worked closely with the owner to decorate the home.

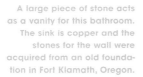

A large piece of stone acts as a vanity for this bathroom. The sink is copper and the stones for the wall were acquired from an old foundation in Fort Klamath, Oregon.

Left: A bathroom off the master bedroom offers a soaking tub and views of the trout pond. The vanity was created from recycled redwood. The floor is complete with radiant heat to warm your toes after a lounge in the tub.

Below: The fireplace in the master bedroom provides a sense of romance. The mantel was created from an old hand-hewn barn beam.

RUNNING WATER

Running Water

I HAD SEEN THE SITE under construction for a few years before I actually visited it. With the home being a few miles off the highway, I had no idea what was being created. The distance obscured things. In time the project just disappeared from view all together. It blended so well with the environment that one had to look hard just to find it.

The owner of the home, a top-notch computer whiz, had walked architect Larry Pearson through the site and had requested an inspirational, three-bedroom complex that integrated the property's hot water springs into the plan. Pearson drew the original designs on a beach in Hawaii. But the design of the building evolved over a two-year period with extensive drawings (from my perspective, Pearson did almost a full set of encyclopedias on this project). The owner encouraged both Pearson and Yellowstone Traditions, builders of the home, to assemble a collection of very talented artists (I don't use that word lightly) to create a world-class setting. In truth, the entire project was organic in nature, and changes were often made on-site. The artists who did the actual work on the building were encouraged to make suggestions and to utilize their creative talents to enhance the uniqueness of the entire project. They were obviously quite successful in their endeavors.

Numerous individuals associated with the project described the experience as "difficult and challenging." Ed Matos, the engineer on the project, commented that the water from the hot spring had to be pumped uphill a long distance in order for it to flow correctly through the home. The septic system was also a long distance from the home and required a complicated mechanical system. Digging a deep well was also necessary to find fresh water for the home.

Apart from enumerating all the technical aspects, it's necessary to offer a personal view of the project. This is not a normal house completed by normal people. The design of the home is stunning, as is the workmanship on every aspect of the entire project. This home represents art at its finest. It brings out and exposes the best of humanity.

Blending masterfully into the environment, the stonework was completed by the creative folks at Big Sky Masonry, with Guy Fairchild as the master mason. The stone is called Harlow rock and was hand-picked by Pearson and others. Pearson's premise was that is was essential to get it right. Called dry stack because no mortar can be seen, the stones were put together in such a way as to blend with the stratified stone geography on the mountains directly behind the home. Almost six hundred thousand tons of rock was eventually delivered to the job site. The tall, vertical slabs are Basalt monoliths from the eastern Sierras. The architect calls the round ball of stone presently on top of a monolith the "eyeball." The entire construction lasted about three years.

This stone slab picnic table came from China.

Descending to the basement level, one navigates this suspended steel spiral staircase. Designed by Larry Pearson and constructed by Custom II Manufacturing of Bozeman, , each stair was made from reclaimed black granite found in China and transported to the construction site. The back wall behind the staircase actually weeps with a thin, ever-flowing veil of water. The stones at the bottom of the stairs are called Harlowtown Moss rock. The lower level contains a heated swimming pool as well as several wooden bridges crossing small streams of running water.

Four views of the large living room complete with massive leather armchairs and sofas. The seating arrangement was constructed in Victoria, South Africa, and covered with kudu hides. The antique dining room set of table and six chairs are Spanish, from the twelfth century. The overall decor is an extensive collection of both African and Asian/Oriental antiques.

Original Navajo chieftains blankets thrown over the oversized couches add color to the setting. The massive fireplace is large enough to walk into. Inside the fireplace is a sitting stone, for cooking marshmallows late at night. The huge hearthstone, which required massive machinery to move, was found on a ranch near Bozeman Pass. Because of the weight of the stone, it could only be transported via Montana highways at the driest time of the year.

The master bedroom is features this bed designed by architect Larry Pearson. Constructed from elm in a modified Shaker style, the bed was made by Abbott Norris. The cabinet at the footboard contains a plasma TV that rises on command. Recycled stones on the floor were acquired from an ancient monastery in France.

The kitchen cabinets, made of cottonwood cut on the property of the owner, were created by Abbott Norris of Missoula, Montana. A wood-burning pizza stove, called an Il Forno, allows the owner to make and enjoy his favorite pizzas! Fossil stone serves as countertops on the island and window bar. Wrought-iron bar stools surround the island. The hanging pot rack was made by Custom It.

Three views of the master bath. The shower head, created by WaterWorks, dumps thirty-five gallons of water per minute, ensuring no soapy residue on users. The paneled cabinetry was handcrafted from elm trees that had died from a beetle infestation. The trees came from Fort Missoula, where interred prisoners from the Second World War were held. The massive black stone that stands behind the soaking tub is fossil stone from Morocco.

This hidden alcove, one of many in the building, is the resting place for an antique Chinese Buddha.

A round kiva room is complete with a triangular fireplace. A kiva is actually a circular meeting room conceived by Native Americans. The entry to this room is covered with a buffalo hide. A Navajo Ganado rug covers the entryway. Many of the statuary items are gods of fertility. The horse is from the Ming Dynasty. The floor of the room came from slabs of stone from the Yang Tze basin in China.

This is the ceiling of the kiva room. The inlaid sticks are red willow.

Opposite: The hallway floors are covered with CVG (clear vertical grain) fir. This high-quality flooring contains sixteen growth rings per inch.

SKI HAUS

Ski
Haus

IHAD VISITED THE SKI HAUS several times
while it was under construction. The home was
designed by Larry Pearson as a themed traditional
Alpine chalet. With deep overhangs, the home
has five fireplaces, including one outdoors, and a hot tub to
sooth your weary muscles and bones after a day of skiing.

And, of course, you can ski right out the back door and return through the front entrance for an afternoon lunch break! The 6,500-square-foot home also includes two master suites, two complete bunk rooms, numerous baths, a game room for the kids and a theatre room to watch the latest adventure movies. It also offers a two-car garage with overhead guest quarters.

Preceding overleafs: Nestled in a grove of tall trees, a front view of the Ski Haus shows the numerous porches and deep over-hangs of a traditional alpine house.

This page and opposite: A variety of views show details of the various porches, staggered and tapered log ends, massive icecycles, the main chimney with soldiers course top, and other archi-tectural elements.

Right: This dry-stacked fireplace was created from Montana moss rock and shows no signs of mortar or cement.

Opposite top: The living room of the Ski Haus allows guests and owners to sit around this massive fireplace. Created by the rock artists at Sandoval Masonry, the fireplace actually has three different fireboxes. A moose head hangs over the mantel. Molesworth-influenced western chairs, leather couches and armchairs, along with Native drums, complete the setting.

Opposite below: A different view of the central fireplace offers a completely different setting. A bison head hangs above this mantel.

A round dining room table is surrounded by chairs covered with soft leather. The chandelier is made from naturally shed fallow deer antlers. The carpet is an Afghan Mahal.

Tucked away in a grove of tall pine trees, the home sits at about 9,000 feet above sea level and offers views to die for! Chris Lohss Construction built it. Monarch Design of Bozeman served as interior designer for the project.

Like many of the other homes I've photographed for this book, I completed making the outdoor images in the dead of winter. And as I approached this home that morning, not only was there six feet of snow on the ground, howling winds and a zero temperature but I also had to stop my four-wheel drive rental car and wait for a herd of fifteen or so bighorn sheep to get off the road so I could make my way to the site!

Above: A view of the kitchen shows a game table set and overhead balcony. The round carpet is also an Afghan Mahal.

Right: A wide-angle photograph of the kitchen area reveals a bar-like setting. The logs used throughout the home were dead prior to being harvested. The logs are sealed with tung oil, which acts as both a character enhancer and a preservative. Elaborate fire suppression systems, fire alarms and electrical wiring are hidden within the logs.

Opposite: The bar stools are from Flat Rock Furniture, Inc., in Indiana. The kitchen cabinets are covered with screen doors. The countertops were created from recycled barn boards. The range is Viking and the French-door refrigerator is Jenn-Air.

The antique European
tall cabinet is complete with
original green paint.

Above: The balcony space above the kitchen serves as both a study and office. The cherry-top desk was made by Brian Kelly for the Ralph Kylloe Gallery and provided for this home through Monarch Design. The carpet is an Afghan Mahal.

Below: In the corner of the downstairs bedroom, a rugged Molesworth western armchair covered in red leather allows a moment of privacy after a long day.

Opposite: This master bath offers a large soaking tub and cabinets with plenty of storage space for all your goodies! The countertop is polished marble.

Left: The upstairs master bedroom has a massive "cattle-baron" king-size bed and a roaring fire to keep your tootsies warm on cold nights An antique European carved red stag deer hangs over the fireplace mantel.

Above: The downstairs master bedroom is complete with working fireplace and two ornate antler armchairs.

SUMMIT LODGE

Summit Lodge

NEARLY EXHAUSTED and out of breath from the high altitude, I drove slowly around each bend. The pine trees that dotted the landscape were small in size, indicating that we were approaching the tree line. From a distance, the home was first just a sliver resting on the side of a mountain.

More cutbacks and switchbacks appeared as I continued to drive. I held my breath while looking over the edge of the mountain as my vehicle inched dangerously close to thousand-foot drop-offs. I had been told that the area was very near a fault line and that it was not uncommon for ten feet of snow to pile up in winter. It was also cold. And windy! But this was Montana.

In time, I made it to the home. At face value, the home is a paragon of symmetry, organic materials and form. I didn't know if I should genuflect or weep in appreciation of its beauty. The dramatic ten-foot overhang, the soldiers course on the chimney, the intricate, natural-looking stonework, the flares on the bottoms of the pine trees holding up the entryway shed roof, the patina on the garage doors, the character of the logs, the rust on the metal sections of the roof, the quality of construction on the hand-hewn notched logs and many other exterior aspects are an artist's dream. It is a noteworthy home.

Designed in classical Swiss alpine style by Larry Pearson, the home was constructed by OSM builders of Bozeman. The owners of the home are well-traveled individuals with passionate outdoor interests, including biking and skiing.

They sought a home with stone and wood in classical alpine design. The house contains three bedrooms and two guest rooms, six and a half bathrooms, kitchen and dining room, living room and exercise area. The home also includes four fireplaces.

Because of the shallow bedrock, it took weeks to get the correct elevation and footings for the foundation. The structure needed to withstand 160 pounds per square foot for the massive snow loads that occur each winter. The home was also seismically engineered by Bridger Engineering of Bozeman to withstand earthquakes.

The wife was instrumental in the interior design. Ninety percent of the furnishings were acquired in Buenos Aires and shipped in containers to the site. The owners' superb taste resulted in a setting that is both subtle and warm, as well as inviting. Monastic in approach, the home is adorned with relatively few accessories. It is not encumbered with clutter.

Opposite, above: The fire-places throughout the home were constructed by Angel Sandoval of Sandoval Masonry, Bozeman.
The andirons, floor candle stand, and chandelier were designed and created in Argentina.

Opposite, below: The dining table, chairs, and sideboard were acquired in Argentina. The stone floor is partially covered with a geometric carpet that includes animal hides.

The staircase was designed by Greg Matthews, from the office of the architect. Extensive use of recycled barn beams adds drama and character to the home.

The kitchen is "country" in design. The soft colors of the walls and cabinets bring energy to the room. The sink countertop is covered with copper and the island top is Noce Classico travertine that has been carefully honed. The floor is made from antique barn boards.

Opposite: View of the kitchen and staircase.

Opposite: Another view of the living room suggests simplicity in design. Smaller rooms such as this one invite and encourage intimacy and conversation.

Left: Another view of the living room with a roaring fire.

Above: The living room is enhanced with light-colored upholstered sofas. Two are covered with light ticking and the other is done in a solid textile. An oriental carpet and Spanish glass-inlay coffee table complete the setting.

This bathroom is constructed with high-character antique barn boards.

Opposite: An iron bed covered with a country quilt sits in one of the bedrooms. Another fireplace by Angel Masonry.

WHITE FISH LAKE CAMP

White Fish Lake Camp

I HAD DRIVEN FOR MORE THAN FOUR HOURS and was hoping the trip would soon end. I had followed another vehicle for hours and, although the scenery was spectacular, I was both exhausted and hungry. Finally, Harry Howard from Yellowstone Traditions, the builder of the home, waved for me to follow him into a tree-lined driveway.

This page and previous over-leafs: Three views of the main home indicate the character of the structure. Dark-stained shingles comple-ment the intricate stonework, which was completed by Jim Boyce of Jim Boyce Masonry in Kalispell, Montana. The manicured landscaping was completed and maintained by Mark Johnson of Majestic Mountain Landscape, also of Kalispell.

Opposite above and below: This stone gazebo, created by Jim Boyce, was built on the site of an old chimney. The stone structure, complete with shingle roof and soldiers course on the chimney, offers oversized upholstered wicker chairs, sofa and coffee table to those wishing an after-noon break.

Opposite outside: The com-pound also offers a multi-vehi-cle garage with overhead apartment. The staircase and stonework add to the rustic ambiance of the setting.

Appearing before me was a very disciplined, structured and organized family compound nestled neatly among the trees. Calmness was the phrase that came to me as we wandered around the property.

Actually, four structures were built on the property. Overlooking an extraordinary lake, a grand stone gazebo was constructed on the waterfront site of an old chimney. A 1920 historic log cabin was removed and restacked on another part of the property. A modern home was then constructed on the site of the original cabin. A garage with overhead apartment was also created on the grounds. The owners of the home, wanting a family retreat, were very instrumental in the design and decoration of the compound. The antique furnishings came from their own collection.

The home, described as "mythic" by architect Larry Pearson, was built for friendship and intimacy. The superintendent for the project was Mike Jones from Yellowstone Traditions.

Opposite: The casual living room centers on this massive fireplace, which was created by Jim Boyce. An eclectic mix of casual furniture rests on a floor of rough-cut antique oak.

Left: Eight Windsor-style armchairs surround the dining room table. An upholstered window seat allows for views of the lake. A wrought-iron chandelier with eight hide shades lights the room.

Below: The sun porch offers comfortable wicker furniture and a fireplace.

Right: The kitchen in the main house has classic country styling. The custom cabinets are made of pine. Metal barstools with wooden tops are permanently secured to the floor.

Opposite: Another view of the kitchen shows the lower cabinets complete with green-painted wainscot paneling. The countertops are granite. An extensive collection of copper cook-ware is professionally displayed on the wall. A butcher block table serves for food preparation. The floors were created from antique rough-sawn oak.

Above: The kids prefer to have their three mattresses on the floor directly under the ceiling fan!

Above right: An ornate iron four-poster bed with luxurious textiles anchors the main bedroom. The doors lead to a balcony that offers exceptional views of the lake. Antique leather luggage rests at the foot of the bed.

Below right: A brass bed layered with down comforters and country textiles makes another bedroom cozy and inviting.

Opposite: A contemporary claw-foot soaking tub sits in an upstairs restroom. The faucets and feet are nickel-plated brass.

Opposite: This 1920s historic log cabin was dismantled and reassembled at another site on the property.

Above left: The guest house living room has a massive fireplace and a pair of covered armchairs for watching the fire.

Above right: View of the living room reveals the staircase leading to the upstairs sleeping quarters. The door leading to the back porch was custom-made by the creative folks at Yellowstone Traditions.

Below left: The iron breakfast set includes four armchairs and a round table. The exposed beams were refinished before the cabin was reassembled. The floor is recycled fir. Slate was used for the kitchen countertop.

Below right: The log cabin reassembled on the property has a back porch that extends the living space with built-in sofas and plenty of throw pillows. Antique wicker chairs complete the setting.

Furniture Builders and Woodworkers

Doug Tedrow
Wood River Rustics
PO Box 3446
Ketchum, Idaho 83340
208.762.1442

Diane Ross
Rustic Furniture Limited Company
PO Box 253
Willow Creek, Montana 59760
406.285.6882
www.rusticfurniture.net

Lester Santos
2208 Public Street
Cody, Wyoming 82414
307.587.6543

Jimmy and Linda Covert
2007 Public Street
Cody, Wyoming 82414
307.527.5964

Montana Craftsman Woodworks
Chris Kurowski
Bozeman, MT
406.522.0181

Nellis Woodworking
Eric Nellis
4470 Amsterdam Rd.
Manhattan, MT 59741
406.282.9049
eric@nelliscustomwoodworks.com

Architects

Dan Joseph Architects
PO Box 4505
Bozeman, MT 59772
800.800.3935
Dan@djawest.com

KMA, Inc.
Kirk Michels Architects
409 East Callender Street
Livingston, Montana 59047
406.222.8611
406.222.6520

Jarvis Group Architects
511 Sun Valley Road, Suite 202
PO Box 626
Ketchum, Idaho 83340
208.726.4031
www.jarvis-group.com

LPAIA
Larry Pearson
777 E Main Street, Suite 203
Bozeman, MT 59715
406.587.1997

LPAIA (Bigfork)
Adam Britt
836 Holt Drive, Suite 308
Bigfork, MT 59911
406.837.0201

Candace Tillotson-Miller Architect, AIA
PO Box 470
208 West Park Street
Livingston, MT 59047
406.222.7057
www.ctmarchitects.com

Pond and Stream Consulting, Inc.
Alex T. Fox, EI
Resource Engineer
626 Ferguson Avenue, Suite 1
Bozeman, MT 59718
406.522.4056
Email alex@pondandstream.com

Contractors
Lohss Construction
Chris Lohss (owner)
Dan Smith
PO Box 556
Gallatin Gateway, MT 59730
406.763.9081
Lohssci@aol.com

On Site Management
Mike Riley
417 W Mendenhall
Bozeman, MT 59715
406.586.1500
mike@onsitemanagement.com

Yellowstone Traditions
34290 E Frontage Rd.
Bozeman, MT 59715
406.587.0968

Elephant Builders
Bill Keshishian
502 S 19th, Ste. 102
Bozeman, MT 59718
PO Box 117
Gallatin Gateway, MT 59730
406.585.4648
elephantbuilders@msn.com

J.E. Simpson Construction
John Simpson
9475 Old Stage Rd.
Central Point, OR 97502
541.855.8733

Lenoch Builders
Tom Lenoch
1035 Blackmer Ln.
Columbia Falls, MT 59912
406.755.7622

Blacksmiths/Iron Workers/
Lamp Builders
Fire Song Forge
Wil Wilkins
5108 Hwy 93
Conner, MT 59827
406.821.3676

Holleywood Metal Products
Joe Holley
476 Fortsville Rd.
Gansevoort, NY 12831
518.745.5702
shanagraham@frontier.net

Kevin Warren
Warrenweld
110 North D Street
Livingston, MT 59047
406.222.0583

Welding and Machine, Inc.
Jeremiah Hillier
28615 Norris Rd
Bozeman, MT 59718
(406) 586-1934

Engineers
Bridger Engineers
Ed Matos
2150 Analysis Dr.
Bozeman, MT 59718
406.585.0590
info@bridgerengineers.com

Electricians
Etak Electric, LLCEd Matos
Emmett KentBozeman, MT 59718
22696 Hwy 12 E
Elliston, MT 59728
emmett@blackfoot.net

Galleries
Betsy Swartz Fine Art
Betsy Swartz
Bozeman, MT
800.585.8339

Fighting Bear Antiques
PO Box 3790
375 South Cache Drive
Jackson, WY 83001
307.733.2669

Ralph Kylloe Gallery
PO Box 669
Lake George, NY 12845
518.696.4100
www.Ralphkylloe.com

Home Entertainment Centers

Thirsty Ear HI-FI
9 East Main Street
Bozeman, MT 59715
406.586.8578

Interior Designers and Decorators

Carole Hamill & Associates
Carole Hamill
16119 Chalfont Circle
Dallas, TX 75248
(972) 239-9385
chamill@secglobal.net

Design Works
Elizabeth Schultz Gerlach
19 W Babcock
Bozeman, MT 59715
406.582.0222
elizabeth@designworksmt.com

Monarch Design Group
6730 Tawney Brown
Bozeman, MT 59718
406.586.5789
monarchdesignllc@aol.com

Peace Design
Bill Peace, owner
Hillary Linthicum, designer
349 Peachtree Hills Ave., NE C2
Atlanta, GA 30305
404.237.8681
bpeace@peacedesign.org
hillary@peacedesign.org

Masonry and Stonework

Angel Sandoval Masonry
Angel Sandoval
915 Jeanette, Apt. D
Belgrade, MT 59714
406.388.0863

Big Sky Masonry
Guy Fairchild
PO Box 307
Clyde Park, MT 59018
406.686.9143

Big Sky Masonry
Phil Cox
505 N 23rd St.
Bozeman, MT 59715
406.682.7863

Gary M. Gloyne
931 Deetz Road
Mt. Shasta, CA 96067
530.926.4418
blacksmith@finestplanet.com

Mark Hanson Interiors
Bozeman, MT
406.587.3557

McCollum Masonry
Jerry McCollum
877 Casino Rd.
Medford, OR 97501
541.779.3757
gmccollum541@charter.net

Set In Stone
Andrew Varela
Bozeman, MT
406.582.2820

Painting and Finishes

Amazing Painting, Inc.
Danny Spain
860 N Meridian Rd., Ste. A4
Kalispell, MT 59901
406.756.0535
amazing@montana.com

Dependable Paint
Ping McKay
8002 Timberline Dr., #1
Bozeman, MT 59718
406.587.2523
ping@dependablepaint.com

Tile, Flooring and Doors, Specialties

Ceramica Specialty Tiles
Bozeman, MT
406.582.8989

Fantasia Showrooms
Tricia Kulbeck
5 E Main St.
Bozeman, MT 59715
406.582.0174
tricia@fantasticshowrooms.com

Montana Reclaimed Lumber Company
75777 Gallatin Rd.
Gallatin Gateway, MT 59730
406.585.9250

Montana Sash & Door
Richard Garwood
18 Peregrine Way
Bozeman, MT 59718
406.586.1858

Montana Tile & Stone
Price Wills, owner
58 Peregrine Way
Bozeman, MT 59718-8113
406.587.6114

Shack Up
Stephanie Sandstone
406.586.6336

Sound Decision
Dallas and Tracey Eccles
101 E. Center St., Ste. B
Kalispell, MT 59901
406.755.7800

Studio AV
Cory Reistad
706 N. 7th Ave.
PO Box 3220
Bozeman, MT 59772
406.586.5593
cory@studioav.net

Superior Hardwoods
John Medlinger
PO Box 4731
Missoula, MT 59806
(406) 251-2272